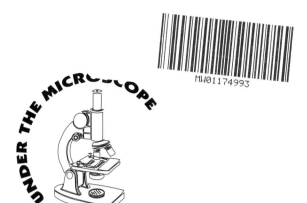

ANIMALS

Casey Horton

Gareth Stevens Publishing
MILWAUKEE

For a free color catalog describing Gareth Stevens Publishing's list of high-quality books and multimedia programs, call 1-800-542-2595 (USA) or 1-800-461-9120 (Canada). Gareth Stevens Publishing's Fax: (414) 225-0377. See our catalog, too, on the World Wide Web: http://gsinc.com

Library of Congress Cataloging-in-Publication Data

Horton, Casey.
    Animals / by Casey Horton.
      p. cm. – (Under the microscope)
    Includes index.
    Summary: Presents powerful jumping insects that live on dogs, the hooks that make a cat's tongue rough, and other microscopic marvels of the animal world.
    ISBN 0-8368-1605-6 (lib. bdg.)
    1. Animals–Juvenile literature. 2. Microscopy–Juvenile literature.
    [1. Animals. 2. Microscopy.] I. Title. II. Series.
    QL499.H77   1997
    591–dc20   96-34483

First published in North America in 1997 by
Gareth Stevens Publishing
1555 North RiverCenter Drive, Suite 201
Milwaukee, WI 53212 USA

© 1997 Brown Packaging Partworks Ltd., 255-257 Liverpool Road, London, England, N1 1LX. Text by Casey Horton. All photos supplied by the Science Photo Library, except pages 17, 21: Natural History Photographic Agency. Additional end matter © 1997 by Gareth Stevens, Inc.

All rights to this edition reserved to Gareth Stevens, Inc. No part of this book may be reproduced, stored in a retrieval system, or transmitted in any form or by any means, electronic, mechanical, photocopying, recording, or otherwise without the prior written permission of the publisher except for the inclusion of brief quotations in an acknowledged review.

Printed in the United States of America

1 2 3 4 5 6 7 8 9 01 00 99 98 97

CONTENTS

FLEA FEAST

Fleas are pesty insects. They are parasites, which means they spend most of their lives living off other animals. In fact, fleas would completely die out if they could not live off other animals. Adult fleas suck blood for nourishment. Each flea has a very sharp tube — called a proboscis — on its head. With the proboscis, it pierces through the skin of a victim and draws blood up into its mouth. A special substance in the flea's saliva travels down the proboscis and into the victim. This substance stops the blood from clotting. Many victims are allergic to flea saliva.

Hard plates, or shields, cover the body of a flea. Notice the flea's sharp proboscis. A flea uses its proboscis to pierce the skin of a victim and gain nourishment.

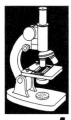

FLEA CIRCUS

• Although they are troublesome, fleas are also amazing insects. They cannot fly, but they can hop and skip in bounds. They can jump distances that are more than eighty times their own height. Try catching one and see!

FOOD'S JOURNEY

The finger-like structures in this photograph are the villi in the intestine of a mouse. The green matter is waste material left over after food the mouse ate has broken down.

In animals, the intestine is where food is digested, or broken down. The food is changed into substances that can be used by the body. The digestive system contains a small and a large intestine. Once food leaves the stomach, it goes into the small intestine. There, most of the food is dissolved into a liquid. The wall of the small intestine is folded — like the folds of a curtain — and is lined with millions of tiny fingerlike structures known as villi. Villi contain blood vessels called capillaries. These absorb the dissolved food, which is then carried in the blood to nourish the body.

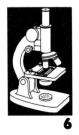

THE LONG AND SHORT OF IT

• In an adult human, the small intestine is 22–25 feet (6.5 -7.5 meters) long. The large intestine measures about 5 feet (1.5 m) in length. In the intestines, food is digested and water is absorbed.

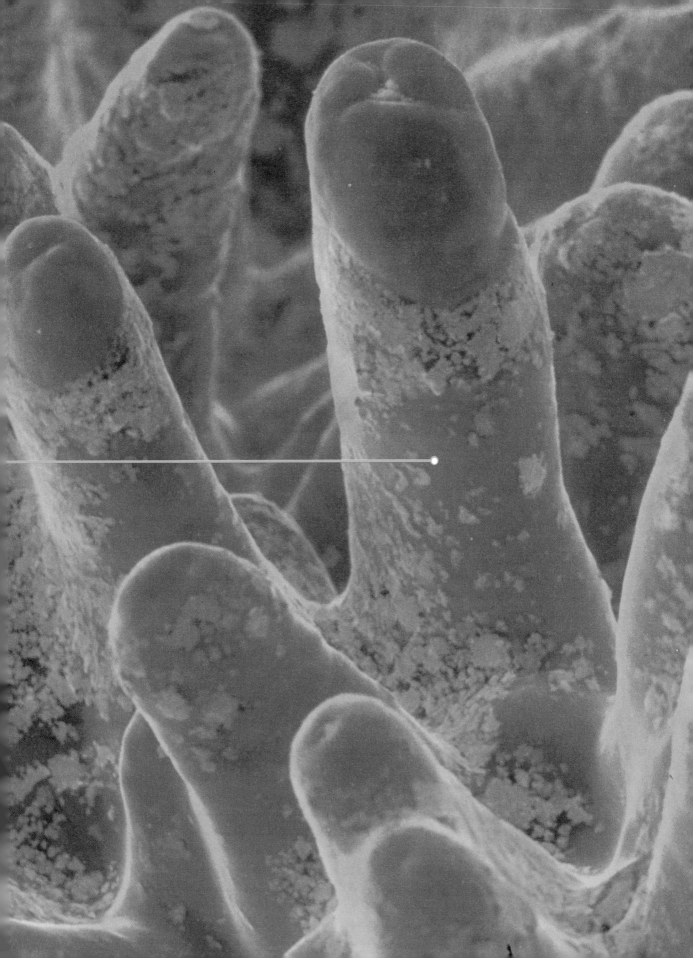

TASTEFUL TOPIC

Most animals have tongues. The tongue is made up of muscles that have various functions. Some of these muscles change the shape of the tongue. Others change the position of the tongue in the mouth. Many animals, including human beings, use their tongues for swallowing and tasting food. Taste buds on the surface of the tongue indicate whether foods are salty, sour, sweet, or bitter. The cells in each taste bud are linked to nerve cells that send "taste" messages to the brain.

Taste buds on this animal's tongue are on either side of a long groove on the tongue. Each taste bud contains many cells. Some of the cells send messages to the brain.

TASTE FOR YOURSELF

• The taste buds for salty, sour, sweet, and bitter tastes are in different places on the tongue. To find out where they are, put a tiny drop of vinegar on your finger. Then touch the tip, the side, and the back of your tongue. Where could you taste the sour vinegar? Try the same experiment with salt, sugar (sweet), and vanilla extract (bitter).

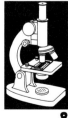

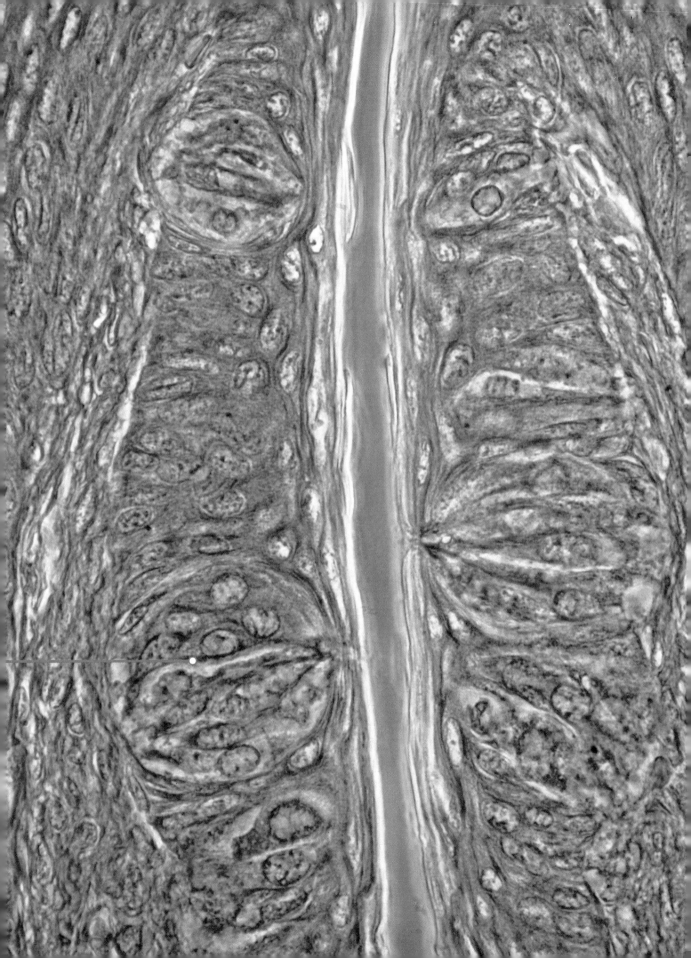

SANDPAPER CLEAN

Cats use their tongues for grooming as well as eating. And when a cat drinks, it curls up the end of its tongue to make a shallow bowl. The cat then moves its tongue in and out of its mouth very quickly. Hooked knobs, called papillae, are in the center of the tongue. When a cat licks its fur, these papillae groom the fur. If you've ever been licked by a cat, you know that the papillae feel rough, like sandpaper. The way a cat's tongue is attached in its mouth determines whether it can roar or purr. Tigers can roar, but house cats simply purr.

The tongue of a cat contains hooked papillae that act like a comb when the cat grooms its fur. If you've ever been licked by a cat, you have felt these rough papillae.

THE CAT'S MEOW

- When a cat grooms itself, it is spreading saliva over its fur. The saliva eventually evaporates, and this helps keep the cat cool. Grooming also releases oils from special glands in the skin, making the cat's fur waterproof.

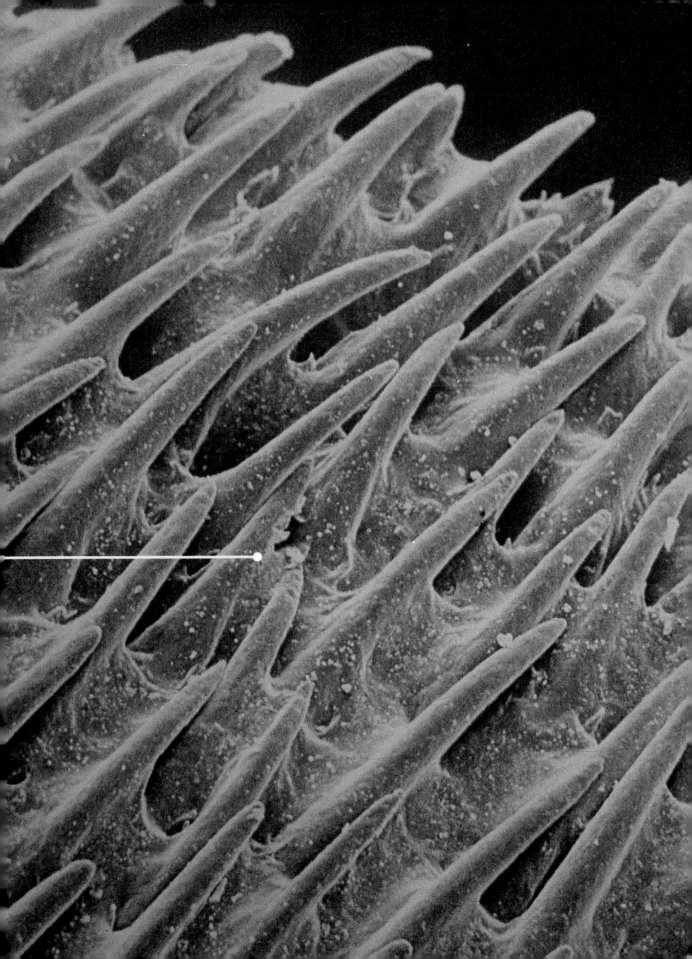

HUNTED HORNS

The pointed horns on the skull of a rhinoceros are not made of bone as many animals' horns are. They are made of a substance known as keratin. In Africa and Asia, poachers illegally kill rhinoceroses for their horns. The horns are sold to people for large amounts of money. In China and other Asian countries, rhinoceros horns are ground into powder and sold as medicine. Selfish actions by humans who kill the rhinoceros or destroy its habitat for their own gain have made the rhinoceros one of the world's most cherished and endangered animals.

The horn of a rhinoceros is a mass of hollow strands of keratin stuck tightly together. The horn is very tough. Human hair and nails are also made mainly of keratin.

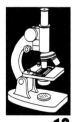

WHAT'S IN A NAME?

• There are two types of rhinoceros in Africa — the white and the black rhinoceros. These names are misleading because both types are roughly the same color — a dull gray.

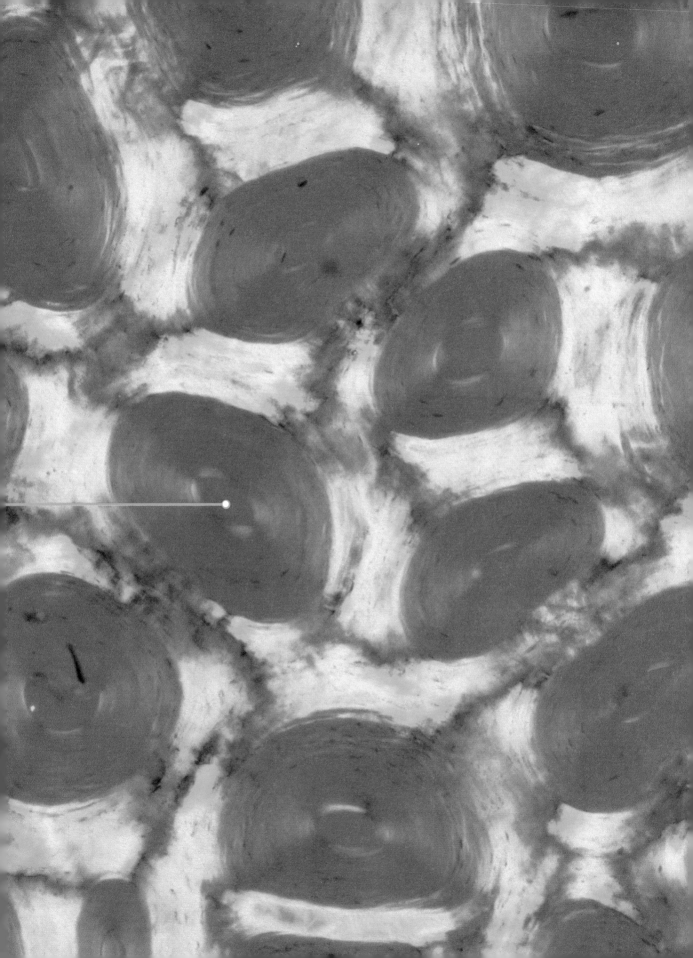

WARMING WOOL

Wool is a type of hair found on sheep and certain other animals. Sheep have two kinds of wool — the thin, soft layer that lies close to the skin, and a thick layer that is on the outside of the animal. The thicker, outer wool protects sheep from the elements and keeps them warm. Sheep wool keeps humans warm, too, when it is knitted or woven into fabric and made into clothing. Both sheep's wool and human hair are covered with scales. Wool scales are pointed and form a honeycomb pattern. Hair has flat scales that overlap each other like the petals of a rose.

Sheep wool is covered with scales. Notice that the scales on this fiber of domestic sheep wool are pointed. The scales fit together to form a honey-comb pattern.

WOOLLY WORLD

• In the United States alone, ten million sheep are raised. These sheep produce 88 million pounds (40 million kilograms) of wool each year. The leading sheep-rearing states are Texas, California, South Dakota, New Mexico, and Wyoming.

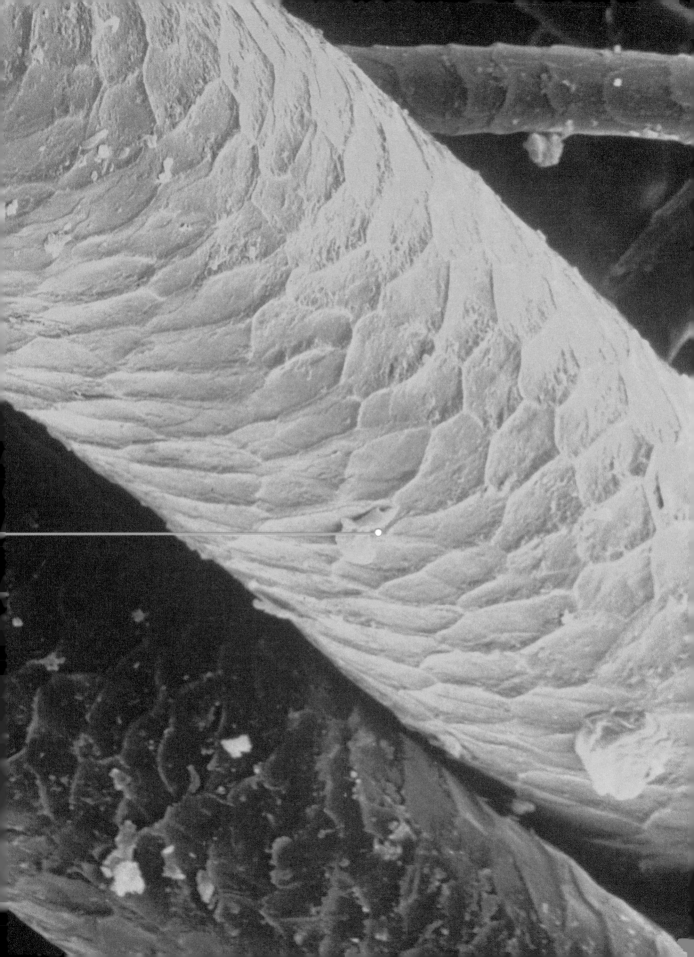

ARMED CREATURE

The English word *armadillo* comes from the Spanish word *armado*. It means "armed creature," which perfectly describes the unique animal known as the armadillo. The armadillo has tough armor that looks like the scales of some reptiles. But the armadillo is a mammal. Its armor is a series of bony plates. There are several plates on the upper body and legs. These plates are hinged together so the armadillo can move. But the animal's belly is covered only with soft skin, making the armadillo vulnerable to attack in this area.

The soft skin of a newborn armadillo soon hardens, except on the belly. The bony plates of this nine-banded armadillo are made up of rows of small segments.

DISAPPEARING TRICK

• The three-banded armadillo is the only armadillo that can roll itself completely up into a ball to protect itself. Other types, such as the nine-banded armadillo, usually flee and hide in their burrows when faced with danger.

TIGHT SQUEEZE

The large snake known as a python does not kill with a poisonous bite. It lies in wait for its prey and then springs out, knocking the victim off balance. The python then coils its long body around the animal it has captured and squeezes the victim until it can no longer breathe. The Indian python lives near water. It is a good swimmer and can also climb trees. Like other pythons, it attacks and eats mammals, such as cats, dogs, and rats — as well as birds, such as pigeons and ducks.

A snake's body is covered with overlapping scales made of a hornlike material. The Indian python scales pictured look slimy, but snake scales actually are quite dry.

DEVOTED MOTHER

• The female Indian python lays one hundred eggs at a time. The expectant mother gently wraps her long body around the eggs to keep them warm for two to three months until the babies hatch. During this incubation period, the mother leaves the eggs only to drink and sometimes to eat.

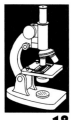

CRESTED CREATURES

The iguana is a lizard. It has four legs and a long tail, and its skin is covered with overlapping scales. On certain parts of the iguana's body, these scales are shaped into crests and spines. The green iguana, for example, has a spiky crest that runs from its head to its tail. Many iguanas also have flaps of skin that surround the head and neck. Most iguanas live on land. Some live in or near forests and are skilled at climbing trees. Some iguanas live on rocky coasts near the sea and are excellent swimmers.

Iguanas do not have an outer ear like humans have. The ear opens directly into the head. The dark area in the center of the picture is the eardrum of an iguana.

FREE-FALL

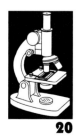

- Green iguanas live in the tropics, near tropical forests. When climbing trees, they often go as high as 40-50 feet (12-15 meters). Sometimes, they leap back to the ground from high branches. Amazingly, they walk away completely unhurt.

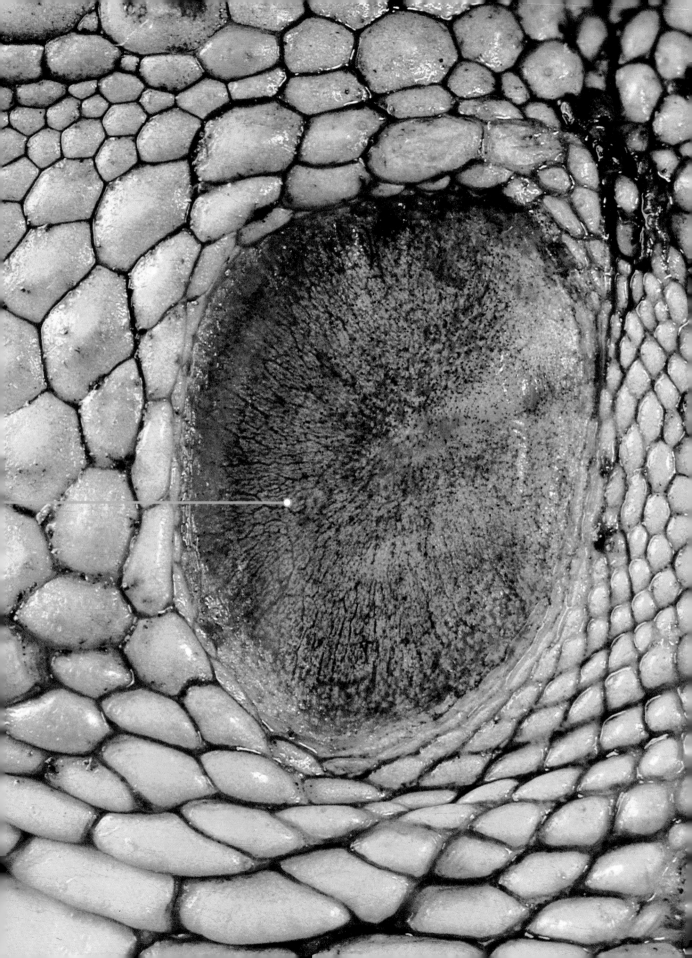

BIRDS OF A FEATHER

People often use the phrase "as light as a feather" to describe how little something weighs. Although feathers are light in weight, they are very strong. The central part of a feather, called the shaft, is hollow at the end nearest the bird's body. The shaft grows out from a small bud in the bird's skin. Very fine parts, called barbs, grow from each side of the shaft. Each barb has two rows of small side branches, called barbules. The barbules on one side have hooks, and the barbules on the other side have grooves. The hooks and grooves fit together to form a flat surface called a vane.

The feather in this picture belonged to a magpie. The thick, blue-gray lines are the barbs. The yellow strands are the side branches of the barbs, called barbules.

A PUZZLE

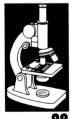

• Which is heavier — a pound of feathers or a pound of potatoes? Answer: They both weigh the same. A pound of anything simply weighs one pound!

22

HAIR OF THE DOG

A dog, like many other mammals, has two kinds of hair on its body. Its long, coarse hairs, called guard hairs, protect the softer, shorter hairs underneath. The short hairs trap air close to the skin, keeping the dog warm. Just as humans lose some of their hair occasionally, so do some other animals. But animals that live in places with hot summers and cold winters lose a great deal of their hair all at once. When winter has passed and the temperatures rise, these animals molt. This means their coats become thinner for the hot summer ahead.

Humans and some animals occasionally lose hair. This dog hair was photographed in a piece of house dust. Dandruff can be clearly seen clinging to the hair.

WHITE, LIKE A FOX

• The arctic fox lives near the North Pole. In summer, its coat is colored grayish yellow. But when the deep snows and deep-freeze temperatures of winter come to the Arctic, the hairs in the fox's coat become pure snow-white.

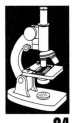

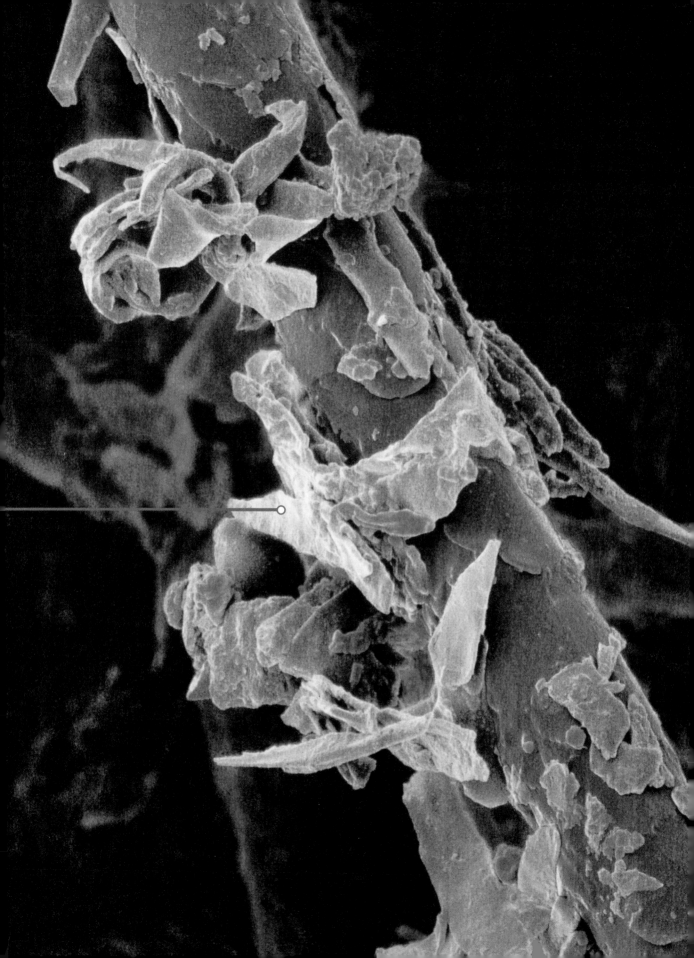

SIGHT WITH SOUND

Although some mammals, such as lemurs and flying squirrels, can glide a long way through the air, they cannot actually fly. There is only one mammal that can fly — the bat. The bat has wings and can fly for long distances. But unlike a bird, a bat has skin covered with hair, rather than feathers. Bats sleep by day and hunt by night. They cannot see very well. They find their way by sending out special sounds as a type of radar. The sounds bounce off objects and send echoes back to the bats. This navigational system is called echolocation.

Bat hair, like human hair, is made of a material called keratin. The hair grows from small pores, known as follicles, located in the upper layer of the skin.

VAMPIRES OF THE NIGHT

- Most bats eat insects, but a number of them feed only on fruit. Still another group of bats feeds on the blood of other animals. They are called vampire bats. After a vampire bat has pricked an animal's skin, it laps the blood up with its tongue.

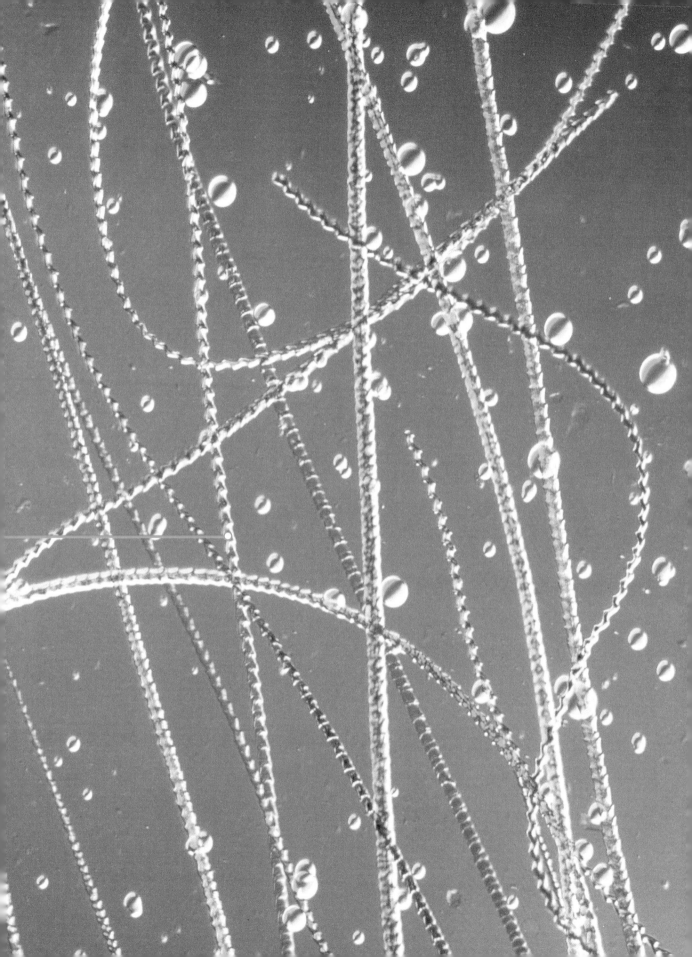

LIFE IN BETWEEN

Scientists divide most living things into two groups — plants and animals. However, there are certain living things that are neither true plants nor true animals. They are something in between. For example, protozoa are some of the most basic life-forms on Earth. Most of them live in water — in the world's oceans, rivers, lakes, streams, and ponds. They feed on waste material from various organisms and on bacteria, algae, and other protozoa. The majority of them move around using whiplike "limbs" called flagella, or with hairlike structures called cilia.

A protozoan *(bottom)* is about to swallow another protozoan *(top)*. The two rows of fringelike hairs are the cilia that help the protozoan to move around.

TRANSFORMERS

• Some protozoa, called amoebas, move in a special way. They can transform their bodies into any shape imaginable. They can even make false feet that help them travel from one place to another.

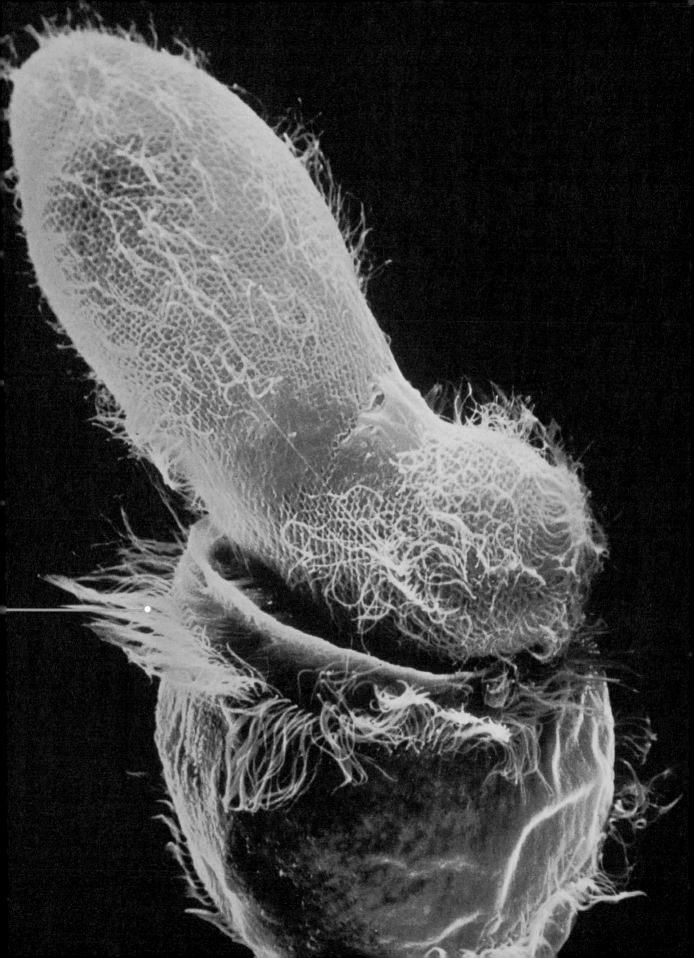

GLOSSARY

flagella: whiplike limbs on the bodies of protozoa that allow these life-forms to move around.

insect: an animal with six legs and a body divided into three parts. It has eyes, jaws, and feelers on its head. Butterflies, lice, earwigs, and flies are examples of insects.

keratin: a tough material found in hair, nails, hooves, feathers, and reptiles' scales.

mammals: a group of animals that feeds their young on milk from the mother's body. They keep their bodies at a constant temperature. Humans, cows, mice, koala bears, and elephants are examples of mammals.

parasite: an animal or plant that lives and feeds on other living beings.

proboscis: a long tube on the head used for feeding. On an insect, it is part of the mouth. On an elephant, the proboscis is the trunk.

protozoa: living matter that is neither plant nor animal in origin, but something in between.

reptiles: a group of animals that relies on the sun to keep warm. Unlike mammals, reptiles cannot keep their bodies at a constant temperature. Most reptiles have scales on their bodies. Snakes, alligators, lizards, and turtles are reptiles.

villi: small, fingerlike structures in the intestine that are essential to the digestive processes.

FURTHER STUDY

BOOKS

Animal Families series. (Gareth Stevens)

Animal Magic for Kids series. (Gareth Stevens)

Cats, Big and Little. Beatrice Fontanel (Young Discovery Library)

Endangered! series. (Gareth Stevens)

Fangs! series. Eric Ethan (Gareth Stevens)

In Peril! series. Behm and Balouet (Gareth Stevens)

Pond Water Zoo. Peter Loewer (Atheneum)

Reptiles. Eileen Spinelli (Forest House)

Secrets of the Animal World series. (Gareth Stevens)

VIDEOS

Animal Babies in the Wild. Animal Friends Video series. (Warner Home Video)

Animals of Africa. Children's Video Encyclopedia series. (Concord Video)

Lakeside Habitat. Animals and Plants of North America series. (Learning Corp. of America)

Microscopes: Making It Big. The Nature of Things series. (Filmmakers Library)

Secrets of Animal Survival. Exploring the Animal Kingdom series. (National Geographic Society)

INDEX

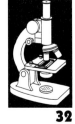